The Midnight Ride

by Amy Ostenso
Illustrated by Marilee Heyer

HAMPTON-BROWN

It was April 18, 1775. Two riders left Boston on fast horses. They rode to Lexington. They had an important message. British soldiers were going to attack!

One rider was Paul Revere. This is his story.

Paul Revere

To
Concord

Lexington

Lexington Road

N

Lincoln

Sudbury River

Waltham

Weston

KEY

★ Start

★ End

SCALE

0   1   2   3   4

Miles

The Colonial Messengers

Before there were telephones, radios, and televisions, people took messages from one place to another. They often rode on horses.

MEDFORD (MYSTIC)

Mystic River

Malden River

Mystic Road

CAMBRIDGE

CHARLES TOWN

WATERTOWN

Charles River

BOSTON

Patriots

Great Britain ruled the American colonies. Patriots were people who wanted America to be free from Great Britain.

It is late in the day. A boy hears the British general's secret plan. The boy tells the patriot leaders. They must act quickly.

It is 10 P.M. The patriot leaders ask Paul to ride to Lexington. That is where John Hancock and Sam Adams are.

Patriot Leaders

John Hancock

Samuel Adams

John Hancock and Sam Adams were important patriot leaders in Boston. They helped the American colonies become a country.

Paul's friends help him get across the river.
They are very quiet. They pass big British ships.

When Paul gets to Charlestown, he meets other friends. They give him the fastest horse in town.
Paul leaves Charlestown at 11 P.M.
The moon helps Paul see.

Paul sees two British soldiers. The British soldiers see Paul.

Paul rides away from the soldiers. Now Paul must go a different way. It will take longer to get to Lexington.

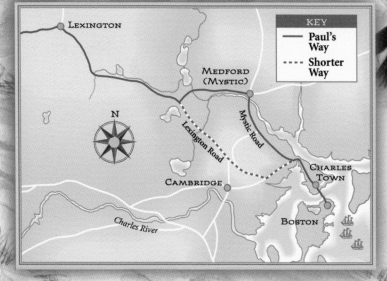

KEY

— Paul's Way

---- Shorter Way

LEXINGTON

MEDFORD (MYSTIC)

N

Mystic Road

Lexington Road

CAMBRIDGE

CHARLES TOWN

Charles River

BOSTON

Paul gets to Lexington at midnight. Paul tells
John Hancock and Sam Adams, "The British soldiers
are coming!"

William Dawes

At 12:30, another messenger arrives. His name is William Dawes. He left Boston when Paul did, but he took a different road.

Paul and William must go to Concord now. The patriots keep supplies there. The supplies must be saved.

A third rider joins Paul and William. His name is Samuel Prescott.

On the way to Concord, British soldiers shout "Stop!" The soldiers ask Paul questions. They let him go, but they take his horse. Paul must walk back to Lexington.

William and Samuel get away, but William falls off his horse! Samuel rides to Concord alone.

Early the next morning, on April 19, 1775, the American Revolution begins. Patriot soldiers fight British troops in Lexington and Concord.

Minutemen

The patriot soldiers were called Minutemen. This is because they could be ready to fight "in a minute."

Paul Revere and the other riders are heroes. Because of them, the people of Lexington and Concord were ready to fight the British soldiers.

Statue of Paul Revere in Boston